Thought-Forms

THOUGHT-FORMS

THE power of thought is a phenomenon for which increasing evidence is being offered by serious researchers. It has been demonstrated that thought can traverse great distances, can affect people and objects, and is indeed a tangible factor in the invisible world around us. The great amount of data in the field of extrasensory perception cannot all be dismissed as superstition, and it is apparent to many people that there is much concerning man's nature which is not explained by purely materialistic theories. There is a need to know the rationale of experiences which lie beyond the readily explainable.

Annie Besant (1847/1933) and C. W. Leadbeater (1847/1934) were both endowed with unusual clairvoyant ability and collaborated in investigating man's invisible nature and powers. In this book they report on their observations of thought power and the forms which it creates. Both were authors of many books dealing with the hidden side of things.

First published in 1901, *Thought-Forms* has been through numerous editions in different languages. It is now published as a Quest Book paperback to meet the increasing interest in extrasensory perception and the accumulating evidence in support of its existence. The book is offered undogmatically as a contribution to man's search for understanding of himself. There are more than 50 color plates and black and white drawings.

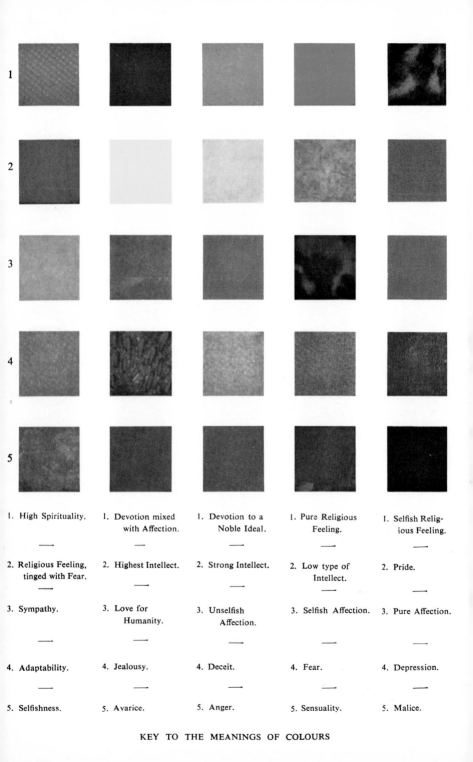

1. High Spirituality.

1. Devotion mixed with Affection.

1. Devotion to a Noble Ideal.

1. Pure Religious Feeling.

1. Selfish Religious Feeling.

2. Religious Feeling, tinged with Fear.

2. Highest Intellect.

2. Strong Intellect.

2. Low type of Intellect.

2. Pride.

3. Sympathy.

3. Love for Humanity.

3. Unselfish Affection.

3. Selfish Affection.

3. Pure Affection.

4. Adaptability.

4. Jealousy.

4. Deceit.

4. Fear.

4. Depression.

5. Selfishness.

5. Avarice.

5. Anger.

5. Sensuality.

5. Malice.

KEY TO THE MEANINGS OF COLOURS

First QUEST BOOK edition 1969 (abridged)
Published by The Theosophical Publishing House, Wheaton, Ill.,
a department of The Theosophical Society in America,
by arrangement with The Theosophical Publishing House,
Adyar, Madras, India.
Fifth QUEST BOOK printing 1986

ISBN: 8356-0008-4

PRINTED IN THE UNITED STATES OF AMERICA

Thought-Forms

By

Annie Besant and C.W. Leadbeater

A QUEST BOOK

This publication made possible with the assistance of the Kern Foundation

The Theosophical Publishing House
Wheaton, Ill. U.S.A.
Madras, India / London, England

PUBLISHER'S NOTE

T<small>HIS</small> book was first published in 1901. Since that time it has been through eight printings in English and has been published in several other languages. It is now offered in paperback edition in slightly abridged form. Some passages no longer relevant today have been deleted and some explanatory footnotes have been added. The main thesis of the book remains intact and the original language of the authors has been retained. The original color plates, painted under the direction of the authors, have been used.

FOREWORD

THE text of this little book is the joint work of Mr. Leadbeater and myself. The drawing and painting of the thought-forms observed by Mr. Leadbeater or by myself, or by both of us together, has been done by three friends—Mr. John Varley, Mr. Prince and Miss Macfarlane, to each of whom we tender our cordial thanks. To paint in earth's dull colors the forms clothed in the living light of other worlds is a hard and thankless task; so much the more gratitude is due to those who have attempted it. They needed colored fire, and had only ground earths. We have also to thank Mr. F. Bligh Bond for allowing us to use his essay on *Vibration Figures*, and some of his exquisite drawings. Another friend, who sent us some notes and a few drawings, insists on remaining anonymous, so we can only send our thanks to him with similar anonymity.

It is our earnest hope—as it is our belief—that this little book will serve as a striking moral lesson to every reader, making him realize the nature and power of his thoughts, acting as a stimulus to the noble, a curb on the base. With this belief and hope we send it on its way.

ANNIE BESANT

CONTENTS

ILLUSTRATIONS

INTRODUCTION

As knowledge increases, the attitude of science toward the things of the invisible world is undergoing considerable modification. Its attention is no longer directed solely to the earth with all its variety of objects, or to the physical worlds around it; but it finds itself compelled to glance further afield, and to construct hypotheses as to the nature of the matter and force which lie in the regions beyond the ken of its instruments. The fact is that science has pressed its researches so far, has used such rare ingenuity in its questionings of nature, has shown such tireless patience in its investigations, that it is receiving the reward of those who seek, and forces and beings of the next higher plane of nature are beginning to show themselves on the outer edge of the physical field. " Nature makes no leaps ", and as the physicist nears the confines of his kingdom he finds himself bewildered by touches and gleams from another realm which interpenetrates his own. He finds himself compelled to speculate on invisible presences, if only to find a rational explanation for undoubted physical phenomena, and insensibly he slips over the boundary, and is, although he does not yet realize it, contacting the astral plane.

One of the most interesting of the high roads from the physical to the astral is that of the study of thought. The Western scientist, commencing in the anatomy and physiology of the brain, endeavours to make these the basis for a sound psychology. He passes then into the region of dreams, illusions, hallucinations; and as soon as he endeavors to elaborate an experimental science which shall classify and arrange these, he inevitably plunges into the astral plane. Dr. Baraduc of Paris has nearly crossed the barrier, and is well on the way towards photographing astro-mental images, to obtaining pictures of what from the materialistic standpoint would be the results of vibrations in the grey matter of the brain.

It has long been known to those who have given attention to the question that impressions were produced by the reflection of ultra-violet rays from objects not visible by the rays of the ordinary spectrum. Clairvoyants were occasionally justified by the appearance on sensitive photographic plates of figures seen and described by them as present with the sitter, though invisible to physical sight. It is not possible for an unbiassed judgment to reject *in toto* the evidence of such occurrences proffered by men of integrity on the strength of their own experiments, often-times repeated. And now we have investigators who turn their attention to the obtaining of images of subtle forms, inventing methods specially designed with the view of reproducing them. Among these, Dr. Baraduc seems to have been the most successful,[1] and he has published a volume dealing with his investigations and containing reproductions of the photographs he has obtained. Dr. Baraduc states that he is investigating the subtle forces by which the soul—defined as the intelligence working between the body and the spirit—expresses itself, by seeking to record its movements by means of a needle, its "luminous" but invisible vibrations by impressions on sensitive plates. He shuts out by non-conductors electricity and heat. We can pass over his experiments in Biometry (measurement of life by movements), and glance at those in Iconography—the impressions of invisible waves, regarded by him as of the nature of light, in which the soul draws its own image. A number of these photographs represent etheric and magnetic results of physical phenomena, and these again we may pass over as not bearing on our special subject, interesting as they are in themselves. Dr. Baraduc obtained various impressions by strongly thinking of an object, the effect produced by the thought-form appearing on a sensitive plate; thus he tried to project a portrait of a lady (then dead) whom he had known, and produced an impression due to his thought of a drawing he had made of her on her deathbed. He quite rightly says that the creation of an object is the passing out of an image from the mind and its subsequent materialization, and he seeks the chemical effect caused on silver salts by this thought-created picture. One striking illustration

[1] In 1901.

is that of a force raying outward, the projection of an earnest prayer. Another prayer is seen producing forms like the fronds of a fern, another like rain pouring upwards, if the phrase may be permitted. A rippled oblong mass is projected by three persons thinking of their unity in affection. A young boy sorrowing over and caressing a dead bird is surrounded by a flood of curved interwoven threads of emotional disturbance. A strong vortex is formed by a feeling of deep sadness. Looking at this most interesting and suggestive series, it is clear that in these pictures that which is obtained is not the thought-image, but the effect caused in etheric matter by its vibrations, and it is necessary to see clairvoyantly the thought in order to understand the results produced. In fact, the illustrations are instructive for what they do not show directly, as well as for the images that appear.

It may be useful to put before students, a little more plainly than has hitherto been done, some of the facts in nature which will render more intelligible the results at which Dr. Baraduc is arriving. Necessarily imperfect these must be, a physical photographic camera and sensitive plates not being ideal instruments for astral research; but, as will be seen from the above, they are most interesting and valuable as forming a link between clairvoyant and physical scientific investigations.

At the present time observers outside the Theosophical Society are concerning themselves with the fact that emotional changes show their nature by changes of color in the cloud-like ovoid, or aura, that encompasses all living beings. A medical specialist[1] has collected a large number of cases in which the color of the aura of persons of various types and temperaments is recorded by him. His results resemble closely those arrived at by clairvoyant Theosophists and others, and the general unanimity on the subject is sufficient to establish the fact, if the evidence be judged by the usual canons applied to human testimony.

The book *Man Visible and Invisible*[2] dealt with the general subject of the aura. The present little volume, written by the author of *Man Visible and Invisible*, and a theosophical colleague, is intended to carry the subject further; and it is believed that this study is useful, as impressing vividly on the mind of the student the power and living nature of thought and desire, and the influence exerted by them on all whom they reach.

[1] Dr. Hooker, London.
[2] Quest Book, The Theosophical Publishing House, Wheaton, Ill.

THE DIFFICULTY OF REPRESENTATION

WE have often heard it said that thoughts are things, and there are many among us who are persuaded of the truth of this statement. Yet very few of us have any clear idea as to what kind of thing a thought is, and the object of this book is to help us to conceive this.

There are some serious difficulties in our way, for our conception of space is limited to three dimensions, and when we attempt to make a drawing we practically limit ourselves to two. In reality the presentation even of ordinary three-dimensional objects is seriously defective, for scarcely a line or angle in our drawing is accurately shown. If a road crosses the picture, the part in the foreground must be represented as enormously wider than that in the background, although in reality the width is unchanged. If a house is to be drawn, the right angles at its corners must be shown as acute or obtuse as the case may be, but hardly ever as they actually are. In fact, we draw everything not as it is but as it appears, and the effort of the artist is by a skilful arrangement of lines upon a flat surface to convey to the eye an impression which shall recall that made by a three-dimensional object.

It is possible to do this only because similar objects are already familiar to those who look at the picture and accept the suggestion which it conveys. A person who had never seen a tree could form but little idea of one from even the most skilful painting. If to this difficulty we add the other and far more serious one of a limitation of consciousness, and suppose ourselves to be showing the picture to a being who knew only two dimensions, we see how utterly impossible it would be to convey to him any adequate impression of such a landscape as we see. Precisely this difficulty in its most aggravated form stands in our way, when we try to make a drawing of even a very simple thought-form. The vast majority of those who look at the picture are absolutely limited to the consciousness of three dimensions, and furthermore, have not the slightest conception of that inner world to which thought-forms belong, with all its splendid light and color. All that we can do at the best is to represent a section of the thought-form; and those whose faculties enable them to see the original cannot but be disappointed with any reproduction of it. Still, those who are at present unable to see anything will gain at least a partial comprehension, and however inadequate it may be it is at least better than nothing.

What is called the aura of man is the outer part of the cloud-like substance of his higher bodies, interpenetrating each other, and extending beyond the confines of his physical body, the smallest of all. Two of these bodies, the mental and desire bodies, are those chiefly concerned with the appearance of what are called thought-forms.

Man, the thinker, is clothed in a body composed of innumerable combinations of the subtle matter of the mental plane, this body being more or less refined in its constituents and organized more or less fully for its functions, according to the stage of intellectual development at which the man himself has arrived. The mental body is an object of great beauty, the delicacy and rapid motion of its particles giving it an aspect of living iridescent light, and this beauty becomes an extraordinarily radiant and entrancing loveliness as the intellect becomes more highly evolved and is employed chiefly on pure and sublime topics. Every thought gives rise to a set of correlated vibrations in the matter of this body, accompanied with a marvellous play of color, like that in the spray of a waterfall as the sunlight strikes it, raised to the nth degree of color and vivid delicacy. The body under this impulse throws off a vibrating portion of itself, shaped by the nature of the vibrations—as figures are made by sand on a disk vibrating to a musical note—and this gathers from the surrounding atmosphere matter like itself in fineness from the elemental essence of the mental world. We have then a thought-form pure and simple, and it is a living entity of intense activity animated by the one idea that generated it. If made of the finer kinds of matter, it will be of great power and energy, and may be used as a most potent agent when directed by a strong and steady will.

When the man's energy flows outward toward external objects of desire, or is occupied in passional and emotional activities, this energy works in a less subtle order of matter than the mental, in that of the astral world. What is called his desire-body is composed of this matter, and it forms the most prominent part of the aura in the undeveloped man. Where the man is of a gross type, the desire-body is of the denser matter of the astral plane, and is dull in hue, browns and dirty greens and reds playing a great part in it. Through this will flash various characteristic colors, as his passions are excited. A man of a higher type has his desire-body composed of the finer qualities of astral matter, with the colors, rippling over and flashing through it, fine and clear in hue. While less delicate and less radiant than the mental body, it forms a beautiful object, and as selfishness is eliminated all the duller and heavier shades disappear.

The desire (or astral) body gives rise to a second class of entities, similar in their general constitution to the thought-forms already described, but limited to the astral plane, and generated by the mind under the dominion of the animal nature.

These are caused by the activity of the lower mind, throwing itself out through the astral body—the activity of kāma-manas in theosophical terminology, or the mind dominated by desire. Vibrations in the body of desire are in this case set up and under these this body throws off a vibrating portion of itself, shaped, as in the previous case, by the nature of the vibrations, and this attracts to itself some of the appropriate elemental essence of the astral world. Such a thought-form has for its body this elemental essence, and for its animating soul the desire or passion which threw it forth; according to the amount of mental energy combined with this desire or passion will be the force of the thought-form. These, like those belonging to the mental plane, are called artificial elementals, and they are by far the most common, as few thoughts of ordinary men and women are untinged with desire, passion, or emotion.

THE TWO EFFECTS OF THOUGHT

EACH definite thought produces a double effect—a radiating vibration and a floating form. The thought itself appears first to clairvoyant sight as a vibration in the mental body, and this may be either simple or complex. If the thought itself is absolutely simple, there is only the one rate of vibration, and only one type of mental matter will be strongly affected. The mental body is composed of matter of several degrees of density, which we commonly arrange in classes according to the sub-planes. Of each of these we have many sub-divisions, and if we typify these by drawing horizontal lines to indicate the different degrees of density, there is another arrangement which we might symbolize by drawing perpendicular lines at right angles to the others, to denote types which differ in quality as well as in density. There are thus many varieties of this mental matter, and it is found that each one of these has its own especial and appropriate rate of vibration, to which it seems most accustomed, so that it very readily responds to it, and tends to return to it as soon as possible when it has been forced away from it by some strong rush of thought or feeling. When a sudden wave of some emotion sweeps over a man, for example, his astral body is thrown into violent agitation, and its original colors are for the time almost obscured by the flush of carmine, of blue, or of scarlet which corresponds with the rate of vibration of that particular emotion. This change is only temporary; it passes off in a few seconds, and the astral body rapidly resumes its usual condition. Yet every such rush of feeling produces a permanent effect: it always adds a little of its hue to the normal coloring of the astral body, so that every time that the man yields himself to a certain emotion it becomes easier for him to yield himself to it again, because his astral body is getting into the habit of vibrating at that especial rate.

The majority of human thoughts, however, are by no means simple. Absolutely pure affection of course exists; but we very often find it tinged with pride or with selfishness, with jealousy or with animal passion. This means that at least two separate vibrations appear both in the mental and astral bodies—frequently more than two. The radiating vibration, therefore, will be a complex one, and the resultant thought-form will show several colors instead of only one.

HOW THE VIBRATION ACTS

THESE radiating vibrations, like all others in nature, become less powerful in proportion to the distance from their source, though it is probable that the variation is in proportion to the cube of the distance instead of to the square, because of the additional dimension involved. Again, like all other vibrations, these tend to reproduce themselves whenever opportunity is offered to them; and so whenever they strike upon another mental body they tend to provoke in it their own rate of motion. That is—from the point of view of the man whose mental body is touched by these waves—they tend to produce in his mind thoughts of the same type as that which had previously arisen in the mind of the thinker who sent forth the waves. The distance to which such thought-waves penetrate, and the force and persistency with which they impinge upon the mental bodies of others, depend upon the strength and clearness of the original thought. In this way the thinker is in the same position as the speaker. The voice of the latter sets in motion waves of sound in the air which radiate from him in all directions, and convey his message to all those who are within hearing, and the distance to which his voice can penetrate depends upon its power and upon the clearness of his enunciation. In just the same way the forceful thought will carry very much further than the weak and undecided thought; but clearness and definiteness are of even greater importance than strength. Again, just as the speaker's voice may fall upon heedless ears where men are already engaged in business or in pleasure, so may a mighty wave of thought sweep past without affecting the mind of the man, if he be already deeply engrossed in some other line of thought.

It should be understood that this radiating vibration conveys the character of the thought, but not its subject. If a Hindu sits rapt in devotion to Krishna, the waves of feeling which pour forth from him stimulate devotional feeling in all those who come under their influence, though in the case of the Muhammadan that devotion is to Allah, while for the Zoroastrian it is to Ahuramazda, or for the Christian to Jesus. A man thinking keenly upon some high subject pours out from himself vibrations which tend to stir up thought at a similar level in others, but they in no way suggest to those others the special subject of his thought. They naturally act with special vigour upon those minds already habituated to vibrations of similar character; yet they have some effect on every mental body upon which they impinge, so that their tendency is to awaken the power of higher thought in those to whom it has not yet become a custom. It is thus evident that every man who thinks along high lines is doing missionary work, even though he may be entirely unconscious of it.

THE FORM AND ITS EFFECT

LET us turn now to the second effect of thought, the creation of a definite form. Students of the occult are acquainted with the idea of the elemental essence, that strange half-intelligent life which surrounds us in all directions, vivifying the matter of the mental and astral planes. This matter thus animated responds very readily to the influence of human thought, and every impulse sent out, either from the mental body or from the astral body of man, immediately clothes itself in a temporary vehicle of this vitalized matter. Such a thought or impulse becomes for the time a kind of living creature, the thought-force being the soul, and the vivified matter the body. Instead of using the somewhat clumsy paraphrase, " astral or mental matter ensouled by the monadic essence at the stage of one of the elemental kingdoms ", theosophical writers often, for brevity's sake, call this quickened matter simply elemental essence; and sometimes they speak of the thought-form as " an elemental ". There may be infinite variety in the color and shape of such elementals or thought-forms, for each thought draws round it the matter which is appropriate for its expression, and sets that matter into vibration in harmony with its own; so that the character of the thought decides its color, and the study of its variations and combinations is an exceedingly interesting one.

If the man's thought or feeling is directly connected with someone else, the resultant thought-form moves towards that person and discharges itself upon his astral and mental bodies. If the man's thought is about himself, or is based upon a personal feeling, as the vast majority of thoughts are, it hovers round its creator and is always ready to react upon him whenever he is for a moment in a passive condition. For example, a man who yields himself to thoughts of impurity may forget all about them while he is engaged in the daily routine of his business, even though the resultant forms are hanging round him in a heavy cloud, because his attention is otherwise directed and his astral body is therefore not impressible by any other rate of vibration than its own. When, however, the marked vibration slackens and the man rests after his labors and leaves his mind blank as regards definite thought, he is very likely to feel the vibration of impurity stealing insidiously upon him. If the consciousness of the man be to any extent awakened, he may perceive this and cry out that he is being tempted by the devil; yet the truth is that the temptation is from without only in appearance, since it is nothing but the natural reaction upon him of his own thought-forms. Each man travels through space enclosed within a case of his own building, surrounded by a mass of the forms created by his habitual thoughts. Through this medium he looks out upon the world, and naturally he sees everything tinged with its predominant colors, and all rates of vibration which reach him from without are more or less modified by its rate. Thus until the man learns complete control of thought and feeling, he sees nothing as it really is, since all his observations must be made through this medium, which distorts and colors everything like badly-made glass.

If the thought-form be neither definitely personal nor specially aimed at someone else, it simply floats detached in the atmosphere, all the time radiating vibrations similar to those originally sent forth by its creator. If it does not come into contact with any other mental body, this radiation gradually exhausts its store of energy, and in that case the form falls to pieces; but if it succeeds in awakening sympathetic vibration in any mental body near at hand, an attraction is set up, and the thought-form is usually absorbed by that mental body. Thus we see that the influence of the thought-form is by no means so far-reaching as that of the original vibration; but in so far as it acts, it acts with much greater precision. What it produces in the mind-body which it influences is not merely a thought of an order similar to that which gave it birth; it is actually the same thought. The radiation may affect thousands and stir up in them thoughts on the same level as the original, and yet it may happen that no one of them will be identical with that original; the thought-form can affect only very few, but in those few cases it will reproduce exactly the initiatory idea.

The fact of the creation by vibrations of a distinct form, geometrical or other, is familiar to every student of acoustics.

A sound plate (fig. 1) is made of brass or plate-glass. Grains of fine sand are scattered over the

surface, and the edge of the plate is bowed. The sand is thrown up into the air by the vibration of the plate, and re-falling on the plate is arranged in regular lines (fig. 2). By touching the edge of the

FIG. 1

plate at different points when it is bowed, different

FIG. 2

notes and hence varying forms, are obtained (fig. 3). If the figures here given are compared with those obtained from the human voice, many likenesses will be observed. The shapes pictured are due to the interplay of the vibrations that create them. Two or more simultaneous motions can be imparted to a pendulum, and by attaching a fine drawing-pen to a lever connected with the pendulum its action may be exactly traced. Substitute for the swing of the pendulum the vibrations set up in the mental or astral body, and we have clearly before us the *modus operandi* of the building of forms by vibrations.

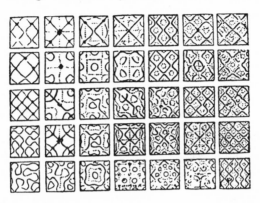

FIG. 3

The following description is taken from a most interesting essay entitled *Vibration Figures*, by F. Bligh Bond, F.R.I.B.A., who has drawn a number of remarkable figures by the use of pendulums. The pendulum is suspended on knife edges of hardened steel, and is free to swing only at right angles to the knife-edge suspension. Four such pendulums may be coupled in pairs, swinging at right angles to each other, by threads connecting the shafts of each pair of pendulums with the ends of a light but rigid lath, from the center of which run other threads; these threads carry the united movements of each pair of pendulums to a light square of wood, suspended by a spring, and bearing a pen. The pen is thus controlled by the combined movement of the four pendulums, and this movement is registered on a drawing board by the pen. There is no limit, theoretically, to the number of pendulums that can be combined in this manner. The movements are rectilinear, but two rectilinear vibrations of equal amplitude acting at right angles to each other generate a circle if they alternate precisely, an ellipse if the alternations are less regular or the amplitudes unequal. A cyclic vibration may also be obtained from a pendulum free to swing in a rotary path. In these ways a most wonderful series of drawings have been obtained, and the similarity of these to some of the thought-forms is remarkable; they suffice to demonstrate how readily vibrations may be transformed into figures. Thus compare fig. 4 with fig. 12, the mother's prayer; or fig. 5 with fig. 10; or fig. 6 with fig. 25, the serpent-like darting forms. Fig. 7 is added as an illustration of the complexity attainable. It seems to us a most marvellous thing that some of the drawings, made apparently at random by the use of this machine, should exactly correspond to higher types of thought-forms created in meditation. We are sure that a wealth of significance lies behind this fact, though it will need much further investigation before we can say certainly all that it means. But it must surely imply this much—that, if two forces on the physical plane bearing a certain ratio one to the other can draw a form which exactly corresponds to that produced on the mental plane by a complex thought, we may infer that that thought sets in motion on its own plane two forces which are in the same ratio one to the other. What these forces are and how they work remains to be seen; but if we are ever

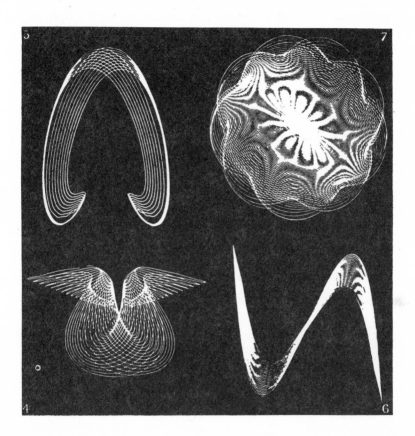

able to solve this problem, it is likely that it will open to us a new and exceedingly valuable field of knowledge.

GENERAL PRINCIPLES

Three general principles underlie the production of all thought-forms:

1. Quality of thought determines color.
2. Nature of thought determines form.
3. Definiteness of thought determines clearness of outline.

THE MEANING OF THE COLORS

THE table of colors given in the frontispiece has been thoroughly described in the book *Man Visible and Invisible*, and the meaning to be attached to them is just the same in the thought-form as in the body out of which it is evolved. For the sake of those who have not at hand the full description given in the book just mentioned, it will be well to state that black means hatred and malice. Red, of all shades from lurid brick-red to brilliant scarlet, indicates anger; brutal anger will show as flashes of lurid red from dark brown clouds, while the anger of " noble indignation " is a vivid scarlet, by no means unbeautiful, though it gives an unpleasant thrill; a particularly dark and unpleasant red, almost exactly the color called dragon's blood, shows animal passion and sensual desire of various kinds. Clear brown (almost burnt sienna) shows avarice; hard dull brown-grey is a sign of selfishness—a color which is indeed painfully common; deep heavy grey signifies depression, while a livid pale grey is associated with fear; grey-green is a signal of deceit, while brownish-green (usually flecked with points and flashes of scarlet) betokens jealousy. Green seems always to denote adaptability; in the lowest case, when mingled·with selfishness, this adaptability becomes deceit; at a later stage, when the color becomes purer, it means rather the wish to be all things to all men, even though it may be chiefly for the sake of becoming popular and bearing a good reputation with them; in its still higher, more delicate and more luminous aspect, it shows the divine power of sympathy. Affection expresses itself in all shades of crimson and rose; a full clear carmine means a strong healthy affection of normal type; if stained heavily with brown-grey, a selfish and grasping feeling is indicated, while pure pale rose marks that absolutely unselfish love which is possible only to high natures; it passes from the dull crimson of animal love to the most exquisite shades of delicate rose, like the early flushes of the dawning, as the love becomes purified from all selfish elements, and flows out in wider and wider circles of generous impersonal tenderness and compassion to all who are in need. With a touch of the blue of devotion in it, this may express a strong realization of the universal brotherhood of humanity. Deep orange imports pride or ambition, and the various shades of yellow denote intellect or intellectual gratification, dull yellow ochre implying the direction of such faculty to selfish purposes, while clear gamboge shows a distinctly higher type, and pale luminous primrose yellow is a sign of the highest and most unselfish use of intellectual power, the pure reason directed to spiritual ends. The different shades of blue all indicate religious feeling, and range through all hues from the dark brown-blue of selfish devotion, or the pallid grey-blue of fetish-worship tinged with fear, up to the rich deep clear color of heartfelt adoration, and the beautiful pale azure of that highest form which implies self-renunciation and union with the divine; the devotional thought of an unselfish heart is very lovely in color, like the deep blue of a summer sky. Through such clouds of blue will often shine out golden stars of great brilliancy, darting upwards like a shower of sparks. A mixture of affection and devotion is manifested by a tint of violet, and the more delicate shades of this invariably show the capacity of absorbing and responding to a high and beautiful ideal. The brilliancy and the depth of the colors are usually a measure of the strength and the activity of the feeling.

Another consideration which must not be forgotten is the type of matter in which these forms are generated. If a thought be purely intellectual and impersonal—for example, if the thinker is attempting to solve a problem in algebra or geometry—the thought-form and the wave of vibration will be confined entirely to the mental plane. If, however, the thought be of a spiritual nature, if it be tinged with love and aspiration or deep unselfish feeling, it will rise upwards from the mental plane and will borrow much of the splendor and glory of the buddhic level. In such a case its influence is exceedingly powerful, and every such thought is a mighty force for good which cannot but produce a decided effect upon all mental bodies within reach, if they contain any quality at all capable of response.

If, on the other hand, the thought has in it something of self or of personal desire, at once its vibration turns downwards, and it draws round itself a body of astral matter in addition to its clothing of mental matter. Such a thought-form is capable of acting upon the astral bodies of other men as well as their minds, so that it can not only raise thought within them, but can also stir up their feelings.

THREE CLASSES OF THOUGHT-FORMS

FROM the point of view of the forms which they produce we may group thought into three classes:

1. That which takes the image of the thinker. When a man thinks of himself as in some distant place, or wishes earnestly to be in that place, he makes a thought-form in his own image which appears there. Such a form has not infrequently been seen by others, and has sometimes been taken for the astral body or apparition of the man himself. In such a case, either the seer must have enough of clairvoyance for the time to be able to observe that astral shape, or the thought-form must have sufficient strength to materialize itself—that is, to draw round itself temporarily a certain amount of physical matter. The thought which generates such a form as this must necessarily be a strong one, and it therefore employs a larger proportion of the matter of the mental body, so that though the form is small and compressed when it leaves the thinker, it draws round it a considerable amount of astral matter, and usually expands to life-size before it appears at its destination.

2. That which takes the image of some material object. When a man thinks of his friend he forms within his mental body a minute image of that friend,

which often passes outward and usually floats suspended in the air before him. In the same way if he thinks of a room, a house, a landscape, tiny images of these things are formed within the mental body and afterwards externalized. This is equally true when he is exercising his imagination; the painter who forms a conception of his future picture builds it up out of the matter of his mental body, and then projects it into space in front of him, keeps it before his mind's eye, and copies it. The novelist in the same way builds images of his characters in mental matter, and by the exercise of his will moves these puppets from one position or grouping to another, so that the plot of his story is literally acted out before him. With our curiously inverted conceptions of reality it is hard for us to understand that these mental images actually exist, and are so entirely objective that they may readily be seen by the clairvoyant, and can even be rearranged by some one other than their creator. Some novelists have been dimly aware of such a process, and have testified that their characters when once created developed a will of their own, and insisted on carrying the plot of the story along lines quite different from those originally intended by the author. This has actually happened, sometimes because the thought-forms were ensouled by playful nature-spirits, or more often because some ' dead ' novelist, watching on the astral plane the development of the plan of his fellow-author, thought that he could improve upon it, and chose this method of putting forward his suggestions.

3. That which takes a form entirely its own, expressing its inherent qualities in the matter which it draws round it. Only thought-forms of this third class can usefully be illustrated, for to represent those of the first or second class would be merely to draw portraits or landscapes. In those types we have the plastic mental or astral matter molded in imitation of forms belonging to the physical plane; in this third group we have a glimpse of the forms natural to the astral or mental planes. Yet this very fact, which makes them so interesting, places an insuperable barrier in the way of their accurate reproduction.

Thought-forms of this third class almost invariably manifest themselves upon the astral plane, as the vast majority of them are expressions of feeling as well as of thought. Those of which we here give specimens are almost wholly of that class, except that we take a few examples of the beautiful thought-forms created in definite meditation by those who, through long practice, have learnt how to think.

Thought-forms directed towards individuals produce definitely marked effects, these effects being either partially reproduced in the aura of the recipient and so increasing the total result, or repelled from it. A thought of love and of desire to protect, directed strongly towards some beloved object, creates a form which goes to the person thought of, and remains in his aura as a shielding and protecting agent; it will seek all opportunities to serve, and all opportunities to defend, not by a conscious and deliberate action, but by a blind following out of the impulse impressed upon it, and it will strengthen friendly forces that impinge on the aura and weaken unfriendly ones. Thus may we create and maintain veritable guardian angels round those we love, and many a mother's prayer for a distant child thus circles round him, though she knows not the method by which her " prayer is answered ".

In cases in which good or evil thoughts are projected at individuals, those thoughts, if they are to fulfil directly their mission, must find, in the aura of the object to whom they are sent, materials capable of responding sympathetically to their vibrations. Any combination of matter can only vibrate within certain definite limits, and if the thought-form be outside all the limits within which the aura is capable of vibrating, it cannot affect that aura at all. It consequently rebounds from it, and that with a force proportionate to the energy with which it impinged upon it. This is why it is said that a pure heart and mind are the best protectors against any inimical assaults, for such a pure heart and mind will construct an astral and a mental body of fine and subtle materials, and these bodies cannot respond to vibrations that demand coarse and dense matter. If an evil thought, projected with malefic intent, strikes such a body, it can only rebound from it, and it is flung back with all its own energy; it then flies backward along the magnetic line of least resistance, that which it has just traversed, and strikes its projector; he, having matter in his astral and mental bodies similar to that of the thought-form he generated, is thrown into respondent vibrations, and suffers the destructive effects he had intended to cause to another. Thus " curses (and blessings) come home to roost ". So long as any of the coarser kinds of matter connected with evil and selfish thoughts remain in a person's body, he is open to attack from those who wish him evil, but when he has perfectly eliminated these by self-purification his haters cannot injure him, and he goes on calmly and peacefully amid all the darts of their malice. But it is bad for those who shoot out such darts.

Another point that should be mentioned before passing to the consideration of our illustrations is that every one of the thought-forms here given is drawn from life. They are not imaginary forms, prepared as some dreamer thinks that they ought to appear; they are representations of forms actually observed as thrown off by ordinary men and women, and either reproduced with all possible care and fidelity by those who have seen them, or with the help of artists to whom the seers have described them.

For convenience of comparison thought-forms of a similar kind are grouped together.

ILLUSTRATIVE THOUGHT-FORMS

AFFECTION

Vague Pure Affection.—Fig. 8 is a revolving cloud of pure affection, and except for its vagueness it represents a very good feeling. The person from whom it emanates is happy and at peace with the world, thinking dreamily of some friend whose very presence is a pleasure. There is nothing keen or strong about the feeling, yet it is one of gentle well-being, and of an unselfish delight in the proximity of those who are beloved. The feeling which gives birth to such a cloud is pure of its kind, but there is in it no force capable of producing definite results. An appearance by no means unlike this frequently surrounds a gently purring cat, and radiates slowly outward from the animal in a series of gradually enlarging concentric shells of rosy cloud, fading into invisibility at a distance of a few feet from their drowsily contented creator.

Vague Selfish Affection.—Fig. 9 shows us also a cloud of affection, but this time it is deeply tinged with a far less desirable feeling. The dull hard brown-grey of selfishness shows itself very decidedly among the carmine of love, and thus we see that the affection

which is indicated is closely connected with satisfac-
tion at favours already received, and with a lively
anticipation of others to come in the near future.
Indefinite as was the feeling which produced the cloud
in Fig. 8, it was at least free from this taint of selfishness, and it therefore showed a certain nobility of
nature in its author. It would scarcely be possible
that these two clouds should emanate from the same
person in the same incarnation. Yet there is good in
the man who generates this second cloud, though as
yet it is but partially evolved. A vast amount of the
average affection of the world is of this type, and it
is only by slow degrees that it develops towards the
other and higher manifestation.

Definite Affection.—Even the first glance at Fig. 10
shows us that here we have to deal with something
of an entirely different nature—something effective
and capable, something that will achieve a result.
The color is fully equal to that of Fig. 8 in clearness
and depth and transparency, but what was there a
mere sentiment is in this case translated into emphatic
intention coupled with unhesitating action. Those
who have seen the book *Man Visible and Invisible*
will recollect that in Plate XI of that volume is depicted
the effect of a sudden rush of pure unselfish affection
as it showed itself in the astral body of a mother, as
she caught up her little child and covered it with
kisses. Various changes resulted from that sudden
outburst of emotion; one of them was the formation
within the astral body of large crimson coils or vortices

lined with living light. Each of these is a thought-form of intense affection generated as we have described, and almost instantaneously ejected towards the object of the feeling. Fig. 10 depicts just such a thought-form after it has left the astral body of its author, and is on its way towards its goal. It will be observed that the almost circular form has changed into one somewhat resembling a projectile or the head of a comet; and it will be easily understood that this alteration is caused by its rapid forward motion. The clearness of the color assures us of the purity of the emotion which gave birth to this thought-form, while the precision of its outline is unmistakable evidence of power and of vigorous purpose.

Radiating Affection.—Fig. 11 gives us our first example of a thought-form intentionally generated, since its author is making the effort to pour himself forth in love to all beings. It must be remembered that all these forms are in constant motion. This one, for example, is steadily widening out, though there seems to be an exhaustless fountain welling up through the centre from a dimension which we cannot represent. A sentiment such as this is so wide in its application, that it is very difficult for any one not thoroughly trained to keep it clear and precise. The thought-form here shown is, therefore, a very creditable one, for it will be noted that all the numerous rays of the star are free from vagueness.

Peace and Protection.—Few thought-forms are more beautiful and expressive than this which we see in

Fig. 12. This is a thought of love and peace, protection and benediction, sent forth by one who has the power and and has earned the right to bless. It is not at all probable that in the mind of its creator there existed any thought of its beautiful wing-like shape, though it is possible that some unconscious reflection of far-away lessons of childhood about guardian angels who always hovered over their charges may have had its influence in determining this. However that may be, the earnest wish undoubtedly clothed itself in this graceful and expressive outline, while the affection that prompted it gave to it its lovely rose-colour, and the intellect which guided it shone forth like sunlight as its heart and central support. Thus in sober truth we may make veritable guardian angels to hover over and protect those whom we love, and many an unselfish earnest wish for good produces such a form as this, though all unknown to its creator.

Grasping Animal Affection.—Fig. 13 gives us an instance of grasping animal affection—if indeed such a feeling as this be deemed worthy of the august name of affection at all. Several colors bear their share in the production of its dull unpleasing hue, tinged as it is with the lurid gleam of sensuality, as well as deadened with the heavy tint indicative of selfishness. Especially characteristic is its form, for those curving hooks are never seen except when there exists a strong craving for personal possession. It is regrettably evident that the fabricator of this thought-form had no conception of the self-sacrificing love which pours itself out in joyous service, never once thinking of result or return; his thought has been, not " How much can I give? " but " How much can I gain? " and so it has expressed itself in these re-entering curves. It has not even ventured to throw itself boldly outward, as do other thoughts, but projects half-heartedly from the astral body, which must be supposed to be on the left of the picture. A sad travesty of the divine quality of love; yet even this is a stage in evolution, and distinctly an improvement upon earlier stages, as will presently be seen.

DEVOTION

Vague Religious Feeling.—Fig. 14 shows us another shapeless rolling cloud, but this time it is blue instead of crimson. It betokens that vaguely pleasurable religious feeling—a sensation of devoutness rather than of devotion. In many a church one may see a great cloud of deep dull blue floating over the heads of the congregation—indefinite in outline, because of the indistinct nature of the thoughts and feelings which cause it; flecked too often with brown and grey, because ignorant devotion absorbs with deplorable facility the dismal tincture of selfishness or fear; but none the less adumbrating a mighty potentiality of the future, manifesting to our eyes the first faint flutter of one at least of the twin wings of devotion and wisdom, by the use of which the soul flies upward to God from whom it came.

Upward Rush of Devotion.—The form in Fig. 15 bears much the same relation to that of Fig. 14 as did the clearly outlined projectile of Fig. 10 to the indeterminate cloud of Fig. 8. We could hardly have a more marked contrast than that between the nebulosity in Fig. 14 and the virile vigor of the splendid spire of highly developed devotion which leaps into being before us in Fig. 15. This is no uncertain half-formed sentiment; it is the outrush into manifestation of a grand emotion rooted deep in the knowledge of fact. The man who feels such devotion as this is one who knows in whom he has believed; the man who makes such a thought-form as this is one who has taught himself how to think. The determination of the upward rush points to courage as well as conviction, while the sharpness of its outline shows the clarity of its creator's conception, and the peerless purity of its color bears witness to his utter unselfishness.

The Response to Devotion.—In Fig. 17 we see the result of his thought—the response of the LOGOS to the appeal made to Him, the truth which underlies the highest and best part of the persistent belief in an answer to prayer. It needs a few words of explanation. On every plane of His solar system our LOGOS pours forth His light, His power, His life, and naturally it is on the higher planes that this outpouring of divine strength can be given most fully. The descent from each plane to that next below it means an almost paralysing limitation—a limitation entirely incomprehensible except to those who have experienced the higher possibilities of human consciousness. Thus the divine life flows forth with incomparably greater fulness on the mental plane than on the astral; and yet even its glory at the mental level is ineffably transcended by that of the buddhic plane. Normally each of these mighty waves of influence spreads about its appropriate plane—horizontally, as it were—but it does not pass into the obscuration of a plane lower than that for which it was originally intended.

Yet there are conditions under which the grace and strength peculiar to a higher plane may in a measure be brought down to a lower one, and may spread abroad there with wonderful effect. This seems to be possible only when a special channel is for the moment opened; and that work must be done from below and by the effort of man. It has before been explained that whenever a man's thought or feeling is selfish, the energy which it produces moves in a close curve, and thus inevitably returns and expends itself upon its own level; but when the thought or feeling is absolutely unselfish, its energy rushes forth in an open curve, and thus does *not* return in the ordinary sense, but pierces through into the plane above because only in that higher condition, with its additional dimension, can it find room for its expansion. But in thus breaking through, such a thought or feeling holds open a door (to speak symbolically) of dimension equivalent to its own diameter, and

thus furnishes the requisite channel through which
the divine force appropriate to the higher plane can
pour itself into the lower with marvellous results, not
only for the thinker but for others. An attempt is
made in Fig. 17 to symbolize this, and to indicate
the great truth that an infinite flood of the higher
type of force is always ready and waiting to pour
through when the channel is offered, just as water
may be said to be waiting to pour through the first
pipe that may be opened.

The result of the descent of divine life is a very
great strengthening and uplifting of the maker of the
channel, and the spreading all about him of a most
powerful and beneficent influence. This effect has
often been called an answer to prayer, and has been
attributed to a " special interposition of Providence ",
instead of to the unerring action of the great and im-
mutable divine law.

Self-Renunciation.—Fig. 16 gives us yet another
form of devotion, producing an exquisitely beautiful
form of a type quite new to us—a type in which one
might at first sight suppose that various graceful
shapes, belonging to animate nature were being imitated. Fig. 16, for example, is somewhat suggestive
of a partially opened flower-bud, while other forms
are found to bear a certain resemblance to shells or
leaves or tree-shapes. Manifestly, however, these are
not and cannot be copies of vegetable or animal
forms, and it seems probable that the explanation of
the similarity lies very much deeper than that. An

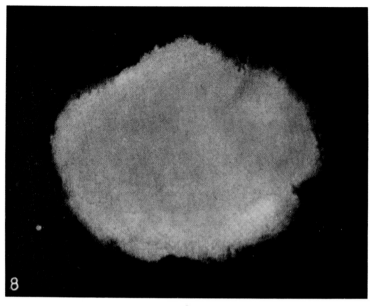

8

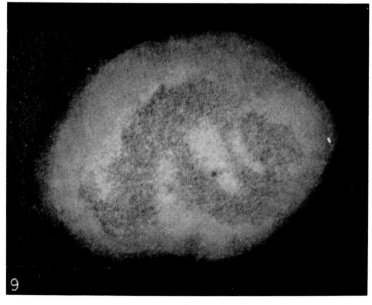

9

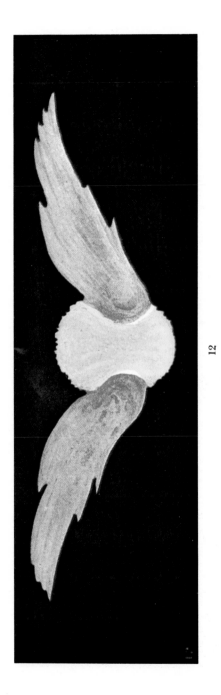

12

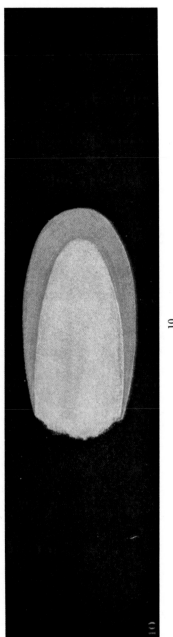

10

11

13

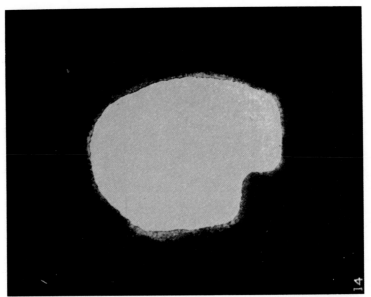

14

16

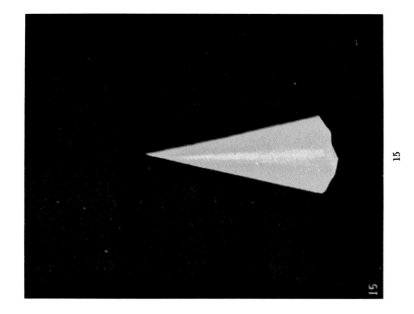

17

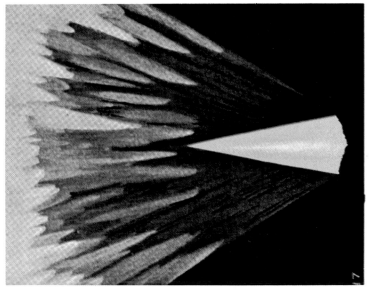

15

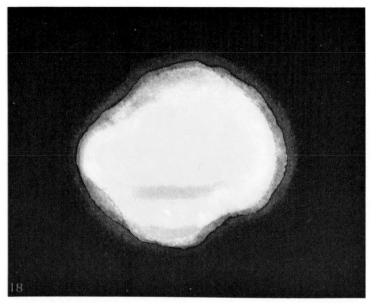

18

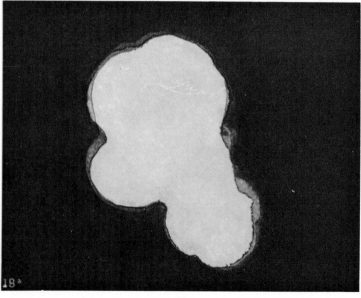

18a

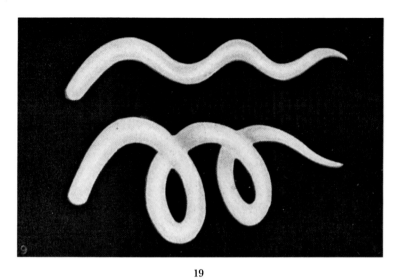

19

24

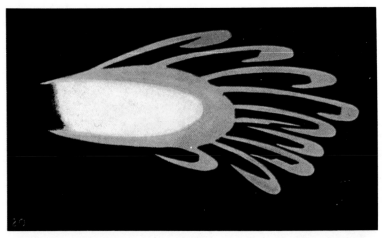

20

21

analogous and even more significant fact is that some very complex thought-forms can be exactly imitated by the action of certain mechanical forces, as has been said above. While with our present knowledge it would be unwise to attempt a solution of the very fascinating problem presented by these remarkable resemblances, it seems likely that we are obtaining a glimpse across the threshold of a very mighty mystery, for if by certain thoughts we produce a form which has been duplicated by the processes of nature, we have at least a presumption that these forces of nature work along lines somewhat similar to the action of those thoughts. Since the universe is itself a mighty thought-form called into existence by the LOGOS, it may well be that tiny parts of it are also the thought-forms of minor entities engaged in the same work; and thus perhaps we may approach a comprehension of what is meant by the three hundred and thirty million Devas of the Hindus.

This form is of the loveliest pale azure, with a glory of white light shining through it—something indeed to tax the skill even of the indefatigable artist who worked so hard to get them as nearly right as possible. It is what a Catholic would call a definite " act of devotion "—better still, an act of utter self-lessness, of self-surrender and renunciation.

INTELLECT

Vague Intellectual Pleasure.—Fig. 18 represents a vague cloud of the same order as those shown in

Figs. 8 and 14, but in this case the color is yellow instead of crimson or blue. Yellow in any of man's vehicles always indicates intellectual capacity, but its shades vary and it may be complicated by the admixture of other hues. Generally speaking, it has a deeper and duller tint if the intellect is directed chiefly into lower channels, more especially if the objects are selfish. In the astral or mental body of the average man it would show itself as yellow ochre, while pure intellect devoted to the study of philosophy or mathematics appears frequently to be golden, and this rises gradually to a beautiful clear and luminous lemon or primrose yellow when a powerful intellect is being employed absolutely unselfishly for the benefit of humanity. Most yellow thought-forms are clearly outlined, and a vague cloud of this color is comparatively rare. It indicates intellectual pleasure—appreciation of the result of ingenuity, or the delight felt in clever workmanship. Such pleasure as the ordinary man derives from the contemplation of a picture usually depends chiefly upon the emotions of admiration, affection, or pity which it arouses within him, or sometimes, if it portrays a scene with which he is familiar, its charm consists in its power to awaken the memory of past joys. An artist, however, may derive from a picture a pleasure of an entirely different character, based upon his recognition of the excellence of the work, and of the ingenuity which has been exercised in producing certain results. Such pure intellectual gratification shows itself in a yellow cloud; and the same effect may be produced by delight in musical ingenuity, or the subtleties of argument. A cloud of this nature betokens the entire absence of any personal emotion, for if that were present it would inevitably tinge the yellow with its own appropriate color.

The Intention to Know.—Fig. 19 is of interest as showing us something of the growth of a thought-form. The earlier stage, which is indicated by the upper form, is not uncommon, and indicates the determination to solve some problem—the intention to know and to understand. A form of this kind frequently accompanies a question, and if, as is sometimes unfortunately the case, the question is put less with the genuine desire for knowledge than for the purpose of exhibiting the acumen of the questioner, the form is strongly tinged with the deep orange that indicates conceit. It was at a meeting that this special shape was encountered, and it accompanied a question which showed considerable thought and penetration. The answer at first given was not thoroughly satisfactory to the inquirer, who seems to have received the impression that his problem was being evaded by the lecturer. His resolution to obtain a full and thorough answer to his inquiry became more determined than ever, and his thought-form deepened in color and changed into the second of the two shapes, resembling a cork-screw even more closely than before. Forms similar to these are constantly created by ordinary idle and frivolous curiosity, but as there is no intellect involved in that case the color is no longer yellow, but resembles somewhat that shown in Fig. 29 as expressing a craving for alcohol.

High Ambition.—Fig. 20 gives us another manifestation of desire—the ambition for place or power. The ambitious quality is shown by the rich deep orange color, and the desire by the hooked extensions which precede the form as it moves. The thought is a good and pure one of its kind, for if there were anything base or selfish in the desire it would inevitably show itself in the darkening of the clear orange hue by dull reds, browns, or greys. If this man coveted place or power, it was not for his own sake, but from the conviction that he could do the work well and truly, and to the advantage of his fellow-men.

Selfish Ambition.—Ambition of a lower type is represented in Fig. 21. Not only have we here a large stain of the dull brown-grey of selfishness, but there is also a considerable difference in the form, though it appears to possess equal definiteness of outline. Fig. 20 is rising steadily onward towards a definite object, for it will be observed that the central part of it is as definitely a projectile as Fig. 10. Fig. 21, on the other hand, is a floating form, and is strongly indicative of general acquisitiveness—the ambition to grasp for the self everything that is within sight.

ANGER

Murderous Rage and Sustained Anger.—In Figs. 22 and 23 we have two terrible examples of the awful effect of anger. The lurid flash from dark clouds (Fig. 22) was taken from the aura of a rough and partially intoxicated man in the East End of London, as he struck down a woman; the flash darted out at her the moment before he raised his hand to strike, and caused a shuddering feeling of horror, as though it might slay. The keen-pointed stiletto-like dart (Fig. 23) was a thought of steady anger, intense and desiring vengeance, of the quality of murder, sustained through years, and directed against a person who had inflicted a deep injury on the one who sent it forth. It will be noted that both of them take the flash-like form, though the upper is irregular in its shape, while the lower represents a steadiness of intention which is far more dangerous. The basis of utter selfishness out of which the upper one springs is very characteristic and instructive. The difference in color between the two is also worthy of note. In the upper one the dirty brown of selfishness is so strongly evident that it stains even the outrush of anger; while in the second case, though no doubt selfishness was at the root of that also, the original thought has been forgotten in the sustained and concentrated wrath. One who studies Plate XIII in *Man Visible and Invisible* will be able to image to himself the condition of the astral body from which these forms are protruding; and surely the mere sight of these pictures, even without examination, should prove a powerful object-lesson in the evil of yielding to the passion of anger.

Explosive Anger.—In Fig. 24 we see an exhibition of anger of a totally different character. Here is no sustained hatred, but simply a vigorous explosion of irritation. It is at once evident that while the creators of the forms shown in Figs. 22 and 23 were each directing their ire against an individual, the person who is responsible for the explosion in Fig. 24 is for the moment at war with the whole world round him.

It is instructive to compare the radiations of this plate with those of Fig. 11. Here we see indicated a veritable explosion, instantaneous in its passing and irregular in its effects; and the vacant centre shows that the feeling that caused it is already a thing of the past and that no further force is being generated. In Fig. 11, on the other hand, the centre is the strongest part of the thought-form, showing that this is not the result of a momentary flash of feeling, but that there is a steady continuous upwelling of the energy, while the rays show by their quality and length and the evenness of their distribution the steadily sustained effort which produces them.

Watchful and Angry Jealousy.—In Fig. 25 we see an interesting though unpleasant thought-form. Its peculiar brownish-green color at once indicates to the practised clairvoyant that it is an expression of jealousy, and its curious shape shows the eagerness with which the man is watching its object. The remarkable resemblance to the snake with raised head aptly symbolizes the extraordinarily fatuous attitude of the jealous person, keenly alert to discover signs of that which he least of all wishes to see. The moment that he does see it, or imagines that he sees it, the form will change into the far commoner one shown in Fig. 26, where the jealousy is already mingled with anger. It may be noted that here the jealousy is merely a vague cloud, though interspersed with very definite flashes of anger ready to strike at those by whom it fancies itself to be injured; whereas in Fig. 25, where there is no anger as yet, the jealousy itself has a perfectly definite and very expressive outline.

SYMPATHY

Vague Sympathy.—In Fig. 18A we have another of the vague clouds, but this time its green color shows us that it is a manifestation of the feeling of sympathy. We may infer from the indistinct character of its outline that it is not a definite and active sympathy, such as would instantly translate itself from thought into deed; it marks rather such a general feeling of commiseration as might come over a man who read an account of a sad accident, or stood at the door of a hospital ward looking in upon the patients.

FEAR

Sudden Fright.—One of the most pitiful objects in nature is a man or an animal in a condition of abject fear; and an examination of Plate XIV in *Man Visible and Invisible* shows that under such circumstances the astral body presents no better appearance than the physical.   When a man's astral body is thus in a state of frenzied palpitation, its natural tendency is to throw off amorphous explosive fragments, like masses of rock hurled out in blasting, as will be seen in Fig. 30; but when a person is not terrified but seriously startled, an effect such as that shown in Fig. 27 is often produced.   It is noteworthy that all the crescents to the right hand, which must obviously have been those expelled earliest, show nothing but the livid grey of fear; but a moment later the man is already partially recovering from the shock, and beginning to feel angry that he allowed himself to be startled.   This is shown by the fact that the later crescents are lined with scarlet, evidencing the mingling of anger and fear, while the last crescent is pure scarlet, telling us that even already the fright is entirely over-come, and only the annoyance remains.

GREED

Selfish Greed.—Fig. 28 gives us an example of selfish greed—a far lower type than Fig. 21.   It will be noted that here there is nothing even so lofty as ambition, and it is also evident from the tinge of muddy green that the person from whom this unpleasant thought is projecting is quite ready to employ deceit in order to obtain her desire.   While the ambition of Fig. 21 was general in its nature, the craving expressed in Fig. 28 is for a particular object towards which it is reaching out; for it will be understood that this thought-form, like that in Fig. 13, remains attached to the astral body, which must be supposed to be on the left of the picture. The thought-form may vary in color according to the precise amount of envy or jealousy which is mingled with the lust for possession, but an approximation to the shape indicated in our illustration will be found in all cases.

Greed for Drink.—In Fig. 29 we have another variant of the same passion, perhaps at an even more degraded level. Once more the hooked protrusions show craving, while the color and the coarse mottled texture show the low and sensual nature of the appetite. Sexual desires frequently show themselves in an exactly similar manner. As men rise in the scale of evolution the place of this form will gradually be taken by something resembling that shown in Fig. 13, and very slowly, as development advances, that in turn will pass through the stages indicated in Figs. 9 and 8, until at last all selfishness is cast out, and the desire to have has been transmuted into the desire to give and we arrive at the splendid results shown in Figs. 11 and 10.

VARIOUS EMOTIONS

At a Shipwreck.—Very serious is the panic which has occasioned the very interesting group of thought-forms which are depicted in Fig. 30. They were seen simultaneously, arranged exactly as represented, though in the midst of indescribable confusion, so their relative positions have been retained, though in explaining them it will be convenient to take them in reverse order. They were called forth by a terrible accident, and they are instructive as showing how differently people are affected by sudden and serious danger. One form shows nothing but an eruption of the livid grey of fear, rising out of a basis of utter selfishness: and unfortunately there were many such as this. This shattered appearance of the thought-form shows the violence and completeness of the explosion, which in turn indicates that the whole soul of that person was possessed with blind, frantic terror, and that the overpowering sense of personal danger excluded for the time every higher feeling.

The second form represents at least an attempt at self-control, and shows the attitude adopted by a person having a certain amount of religious feeling. The thinker is seeking solace in prayer, and endeavoring in this way to overcome her fear. This is indicated by the point of greyish-blue which lifts itself hesitatingly upwards; the color shows, however, that the effort is but partially successful, and we see also from the lower part of the thought-form, with its irregular outline and its falling fragments, that there is in reality almost as much fright here as in the other case. But at least this woman has had presence of mind enough to remember that she ought to pray, and is trying to imagine that she is not afraid as she

does it, whereas in the other case there was absolutely
no thought beyond selfish terror. The one retains
some possibility of regaining self-control; the other
is a slave to overwhelming emotion.

A very striking contrast to the weakness shown
in these two forms is the splendid strength and decision
of the third. Here we have no amorphous mass with
quivering lines and explosive fragments, but a powerful, clear-cut and definite thought, obviously full of
force and resolution. For this is the thought of the
officer in charge—the man responsible for the lives
and the safety of the passengers, and he rises to the
emergency in a most satisfactory manner. It does
not even occur to him to feel the least shadow of
fear; he has no time for that. Though the scarlet
of the sharp point of his weapon-like thought-form
shows anger that the accident should have happened,
the bold curve of orange immediately above it betokens
perfect self-confidence and certainty of his power to
deal with the difficulty. The brilliant yellow implies
that his intellect is already at work upon the problem,
while the green which runs side by side with it denotes
the sympathy which he feels for those whom he intends
to save. A very striking and instructive group of
thought-forms.

On the First Night.—Fig. 31 is also an interesting
specimen—perhaps unique—for it represents the
thought-form of an actor while waiting to go upon the
stage for a " first-night " performance. The broad band
of orange in the centre is very clearly defined, and is

the expression of a well-founded self-confidence—the realization of many previous successes, and the reasonable expectation that on this occasion another will be added to the list. Yet in spite of this there is a good deal of unavoidable uncertainty as to how this new play may strike the public, and on the whole the doubt and fear overbalance the certainty and pride, for there is more of the pale grey than of the orange, and the whole thought-form vibrates like a flag flapping in a gale of wind. It will be noted that while the outline of the orange is exceedingly clear and definite, that of the grey is much vaguer.

The Gamblers.—The forms shown in Fig. 32 were observed simultaneously at a great gambling-house. Both represent some of the worst of human passions, and there is little to choose between them, although they represent the feelings of the successful and the unsuccessful gambler respectively. The lower form has a strong resemblance to a lurid and gleaming eye, though this must be simply a coincidence, for when we analyze it we find that its constituent parts and colors can be accounted for without difficulty. The background of the whole thought is an irregular cloud of deep depression, heavily marked by the dull brown-grey of selfishness and the livid hue of fear. In the centre we find a clearly-marked scarlet ring showing deep anger and resentment at the hostility of fate, and within that is a sharply outlined circle of black expressing the hatred of the ruined man for those who have won his money. The man who can send forth such a thought-form as this is surely in imminent danger, for he has evidently descended into the very depths of despair, so that he would be by no means unlikely to resort to the imaginary refuge of suicide, only to find on awakening into astral life that he had changed his condition for the worse instead of for better, as the suicide always does, since his action cuts him off from the happiness and peace which usually follow death.

The upper form represents a state of mind which is perhaps even more harmful in its effects, for this is the gloating of the successful gambler. Here the outline is perfectly definite, and the man's resolution to persist in his course is unmistakable. The broad band of orange in the centre shows very clearly that although when the man loses he may curse the inconstancy of fate, when he wins he attributes his success entirely to his own genius. Probably he has invented some system to which he pins his faith, and of which he is inordinately proud. But it will be noticed that on each side of the orange comes a hard line of selfishness, and we see how this in turn melts into avarice and becomes a mere animal greed of possession, which is also so clearly expressed by the claw-like extremities of the thought-form.

At a Street Accident.—Fig. 33 is instructive as showing the various forms which the same feelings may take in different individuals. These two evidences of emotion were seen simultaneously among the spectators of a street accident—a case in which someone was knocked down and slightly injured by a passing vehicle. The persons who generated these two thought-forms were both animated by affectionate interest in the victim and deep compassion for his suffering, and so their thought-forms exhibited exactly the same colors, although the outlines are absolutely unlike. The one over whom floats that vague sphere of cloud is thinking " Poor fellow, how sad! " while he who gives birth to that sharply-defined disc is already rushing forward to see in what way he can be of assistance. The one is a dreamer, though of acute sensibilities; the other is a man of action.

At a Funeral.—In Fig. 34 we have an exceedingly striking example of the advantage of knowledge, of the fundamental change produced in the man's attitude of mind by a clear understanding of the great laws of nature under which we live. Utterly different as they are in every respect of color and form and meaning, these two thought-forms were seen simultaneously, and they represent two points of view with regard to the same occurrence. They were observed at a funeral, and they exhibit the feelings evoked in the minds of two of the " mourners " by the contemplation of death. The thinkers stood in the same relation to the dead man, but while one of them was steeped in ignorance with regard to super-physical life, the other had the advantage of Theosophy. In the thought of the former we see expressed nothing but profound depression, fear and selfishness. The fact that death has approached so near has evidently evoked in the mind of the mourner the thought that it may one day come to him also, and the anticipation of this is very terrible to him; but since he does not know what it is that he fears, the clouds in which his feeling is manifested are appropriately vague. His only definite sensations are despair and the sense of his personal loss, and these declare themselves in regular bands of brown-grey and leaden grey, while the very curious downward protrusion, which actually descends into the grave and enfolds the coffin, is an expression of strong selfish desire to draw the dead man back into physical life.

It is refreshing to turn from this gloomy picture to the wonderfully different effect produced by the very same circumstances upon the mind of the man who comprehends the facts of the case. It will be observed that the two have no single emotion in common; in the former case all was despondency and horror, while in this case we find none but the highest and most beautiful sentiments. At the base of the thought-form we find a full expression of deep sympathy, the lighter green indicating appreciation of the suffering of the mourners and condolence with them, while the band of deeper green shows the attitude of the thinker toward the dead man himself. The deep rose-color exhibits affection towards both, the dead and the living, while the upper part of the cone and the stars which rise from it testify to the feeling aroused within the thinker by the consideration of the subject of death, the blue expressing its devotional aspect, while the violet shows the thought of, and the power to respond to, a noble ideal, and the golden stars denote the spiritual aspirations which its contemplation calls forth. The band of clear yellow which is seen in the centre of this thought-form is very significant, as indicating that the man's whole attitude is based upon and prompted by his intellectual comprehension of this situation, and this is also shown by the regularity of the arrangement of the colors and the definiteness of the lines of demarcation between them.

The comparison between the two illustrations shown in this plate is surely a very impressive testimony to the value of the knowledge given by the *theosophical teaching*. Undoubtedly this knowledge takes away all fear of death, and makes life easier to live because we understand its object and its end, and we realize that death is a perfectly natural incident in its course, a necessary step in our evolution. There is no gloomy impenetrable abyss beyond the grave, but instead of that a world of life and light which may be known to us as clearly and fully and accurately as this physical world in which we live now. We have created the gloom and the horror for ourselves, like children who frighten themselves with ghastly stories, and we have only to study the facts of the case, and all these artificial clouds will roll away at once. We have an evil heredity behind us in this matter, for we have inherited all kinds of funeral horrors from our forefathers, and so we are used to them, and we do

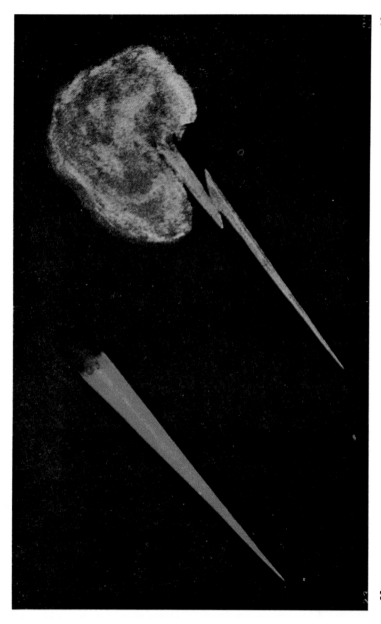

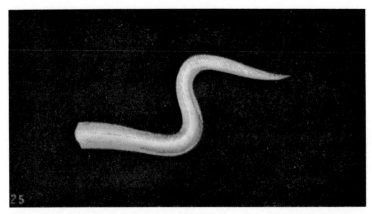

25

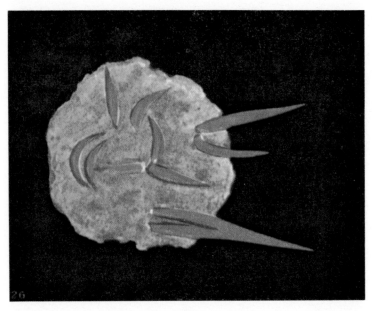

26

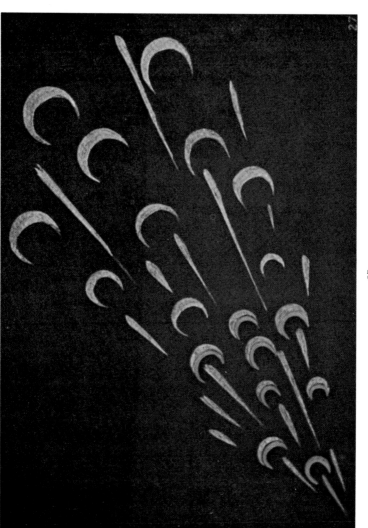

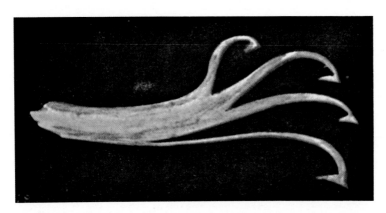

28

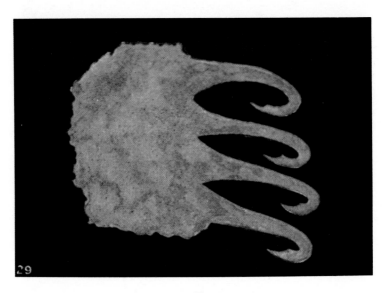

29

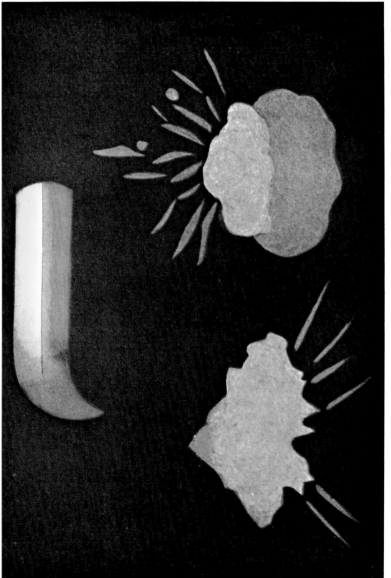

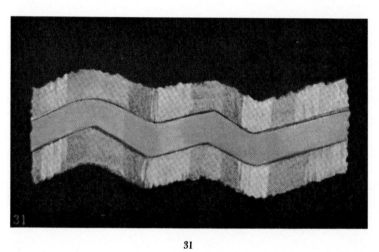

31

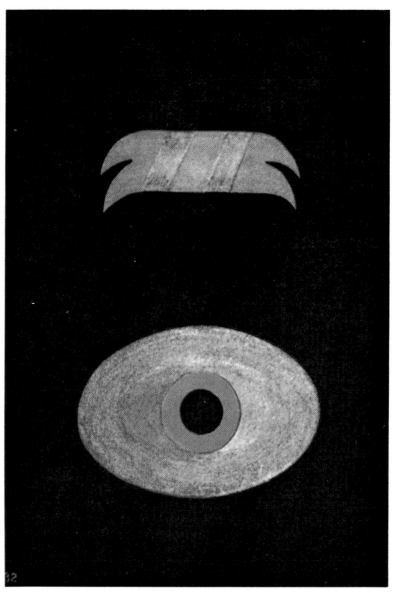

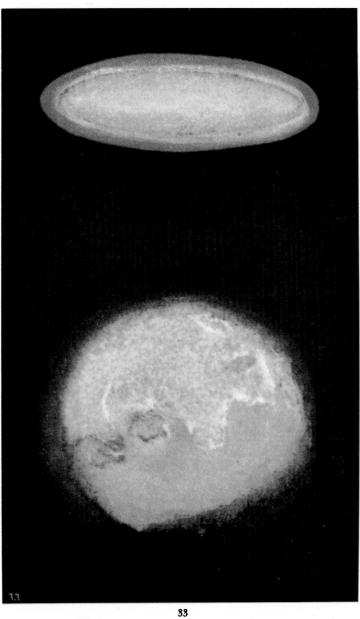

not see the absurdity and the monstrosity of them. The ancients were in this respect wiser than we, for they did not associate all this phantasmagoria of gloom with the death of the body—partly perhaps because they had a much more rational method of disposing of the body—a method which was not only infinitely better for the dead man and more healthy for the living, but was also free from the gruesome suggestions connected with slow decay. They knew much more about death in those days, and because they knew more they mourned less.

On Meeting a Friend.—Fig. 35 gives us an example of a good, clearly-defined and expressive thought-form, with each color well marked off from the others. It represents the feeling of a man upon meeting a friend from whom he has been long separated. The convex surface of the crescent is nearest to the thinker, and its two arms stretch out towards the approaching friend as if to embrace him. The rose color naturally betokens the affection felt, the light green shows the depth of the sympathy which exists, and the clear yellow is a sign of the intellectual pleasure with which the creator of the thought anticipates the revival of delightful reminiscences of days long gone by.

The Appreciation of a Picture.—In Fig. 36 we have a somewhat complex thought-form representing the delighted appreciation of a beautiful picture upon a religious subject. The strong pure yellow marks the beholder's enthusiastic recognition of the technical skill of the artist, while all the other colors are expressions of the various emotions evoked within him by the examination of so glorious a work of art. Green shows his sympathy with the central figure in the picture, deep devotion appears not only in the broad band of blue, but also in the outline of the entire figure, while the violet tells us that the picture has raised the man's thought to the contemplation of a lofty ideal, and has made him, at least for the time, capable of responding to it. We have here the first specimen of an interesting class of thought-forms of which we shall find abundant examples later—that in which light of one color shines out through a network of lines of some quite different hue. It will be noted that in this case from the mass of violet there rise many wavy lines which flow like rivulets over a golden plain; and this makes it clear that the loftiest aspiration is by no means vague, but is thoroughly supported by an intellectual grasp of the situation and a clear comprehension of the method by which it can be put into effect.

FORMS SEEN IN THOSE MEDITATING

Sympathy and Love for All.—Hitherto we have been dealing chiefly with forms which are the expression of emotion, or of such thought as is aroused within the mind by external circumstances. We have now to consider some of those caused by thoughts which arise from within—forms generated during meditation—each being the effect produced by a conscious effort on the part of the thinker to form a certain conception, or to put himself into a certain attitude. Naturally such thoughts are definite, for the man who trains himself in this way learns how to think with clearness and precision, and the development of his power in this direction shows itself in the beauty and regularity of the shapes produced. In this case we have the result of an endeavor on the part of the thinker to put himself into an attitude of sympathy and love toward all mankind, and thus we have a series of graceful lines of the luminous green of sympathy with the strong roseate glow of affection shining out between them (Fig. 37). The lines are still sufficiently broad and wide apart to be easily drawn; but in some of the higher examples of thought-forms of this type the lines are so fine and so close that no human hand can represent them as they really are. The outline of this thought-form is that of a leaf, yet its shape and the curve of its lines are more suggestive of a certain kind of shell, so that this is another example of the approximation to forms seen in physical nature which we noted in commenting upon Fig. 16.

An Aspiration to Enfold All.—In Fig. 38 we have a far more developed example of the same type. This form was generated by one who was trying, while sitting in meditation, to fill his mind with an aspiration to enfold all mankind in order to draw them upward toward the high ideal which shone so clearly before his eyes. Therefore it is that the form which he produces seems to rush out from him, to curve round upon itself, and to return to its base; therefore it is that the marvellously fine lines are drawn in lovely luminous violet, and that from within the form there shines out a glorious golden light which it is unfortunately quite impossible to reproduce. For the truth is that all these apparently intricate lines are in reality only one line circling round the form again with unwearied patience and wonderful accuracy. It is scarcely possible that any human hand could make such a drawing as this on this scale, and in any case the effect of its colors could not be shown, for it will be seen by experiment that if an attempt be made to draw fine violet lines close together upon a yellow background a grey effect at once appears, and all likeness to the original is destroyed. But what cannot be done by hand may sometimes be achieved by the superior accuracy and delicacy of a machine, and it is in this way that the drawing was made from which our illustration is reproduced—with some attempt to represent the color effect as well as the wonderful delicacy of the lines and curves.

In the Six Directions.—The form represented in Fig. 39 is the result of another endeavor to extend love and sympathy in all directions—an effort almost precisely similar to that which gave birth to Fig. 37, though the effect seems so different. The reasons for this variety and for the curious shape taken in this case constitute a very interesting illustration of the way in which thought-forms grow. It will be seen that in this instance the thinker displays considerable devotional feeling, and has also made an intellectual effort to grasp the conditions necessary for the realization of his wishes, and the blue and yellow colors remain as evidence of this. Originally this thought-form was circular, and the dominant idea evidently was that the green of sympathy should be upon the outside, facing in all directions, as it were, and that love should lie at the center and heart of the thought and direct its outgoing energies. But the maker of this thought-form had been reading Hindu books, and his modes of thought had been greatly influenced by them. Students of Oriental literature will be aware that the Hindu speaks, not of four directions (north, east, south and west), as we do, but always of six, since he very sensibly includes the zenith and the nadir. Our friend was imbued from his reading with the idea that he should pour forth his love and sympathy " in the six directions "; but since he did not accurately understand what the six directions are, he directed his stream of affection towards six equidistant points in his circle. The outrushing streams altered the shape of the outlying lines which he had already built up, and so instead of having a circle as a section of this thought-form, we have this curious hexagon with its inward-curving sides. We see thus how faithfully every thought-form records the exact process of its upbuilding, registering ineffaceably even the errors of its construction.

An Intellectual Conception of Cosmic Order.—In Fig. 40 we have the effect of an attempt to attain an intellectual conception of cosmic order. The thinker endeavors to think of the action of spirit upon matter. Here we have an upward-pointing triangle signifying the three-fold aspect of the Spirit, interlaced with the downward-pointing triangle, which indicates matter with its three inherent qualities. It is noteworthy that in this case the thinker is so entirely occupied with the intellectual endeavor, that no color but yellow is exhibited within the form. There is no room as yet for emotions of devotion, of wonder, or of admiration; the idea which he wishes to realize fills his mind entirely, to the exclusion of all else. Still the definiteness of the outline as it stands out against its background of rays shows that he has achieved a high measure of success.

The Logos as Manifested in Man.—We are now coming to a series of thoughts which are among the very highest the human mind can form, when in meditation upon the divine source of its being. When the man in reverent contemplation tries to raise his thought towards the LOGOS of our solar system, he naturally makes no attempt to image to himself that august Being; nor does he think of Him as in any way possessing such form as we can comprehend. Nevertheless such thoughts build forms for themselves in the matter of the mental plane; and it will be of interest for us to examine those forms. In our illustration in Fig. 41 we have a thought of the LOGOS as manifested in man, with the devotional aspiration that He may thus be manifested through the thinker. It is this devotional feeling which gives the pale blue tinge to the five-pointed star, and its shape is significant, since it has been employed for many ages as a symbol of God manifested in man. The thinker may perhaps have been a Freemason, and his knowledge of the symbolism employed by that body may have had its share in the shaping of the star. It will be seen that the star is surrounded by bright yellow rays shining out amidst a cloud of glory, which denotes not only the reverential understanding of the surpassing glory of the Deity, but also a distinct intellectual effort in addition to the outpouring of devotion.

The Logos Pervading All.—Our next three Figures are devoted to the effort to represent a thought of a very high type—an endeavor to think of the LOGOS as pervading all nature. Here again, as in Fig. 38, it is impossible to give a full reproduction, and we must call upon our readers for an effort of the imagination which shall to some extent supplement the deficiencies of the arts of drawing and printing. The golden ball depicted in Fig. 42 must be thought of as inside the other ball of delicate lines (blue in color) which is drawn in Fig. 44. Any effort to place the colors in such intimate juxtaposition on the physical plane results simply in producing a green blur, so that the whole character of the thought-form is lost. It is only by means of the machine before mentioned that it is at all possible to represent the grace and the delicacy of the lines. As before, a single line produces all the wonderful tracery of Fig. 44, and the effect of the four radiating lines making a sort of cross of light is merely due to the fact that the curves are not really concentric, although at first sight they appear to be so.

Another Conception.—Fig. 45 exhibits the form produced by another person when trying to hold exactly the same thought. Here also we have an amazing complexity of almost inconceivably delicate blue lines, and here also our imagination must be called upon to insert the golden globe from Fig. 42, so that its glory may shine through at every point. Here also, as in Fig. 44, we have that curious and beautiful pattern, resembling somewhat the damascening on ancient Oriental swords, or that which is seen upon watered silk or *moire antique.* When this form is drawn by the pendulum, the pattern is not in any way intentionally produced, but simply comes as a consequence of the crossing of the innumerable microscopically fine lines. It is evident that the thinker who created the form upon Fig. 44 must have held in his mind most prominently the unity of the LOGOS, while he who generated the form in Fig. 45 has as clearly in mind the subordinate centers through which the divine life pours forth, and many of these subordinate centers have accordingly represented themselves in the thought-form.

The Threefold Manifestation.—When the form employed in Fig. 46 was made, its creator was endeavoring to think of the LOGOS in His threefold manifestation. The vacant space in the centre of the form was a blinding glow of yellow light, and this clearly typified the First Aspect, while the Second was symbolized by the broad ring of closely-knitted and almost bewildering lines which surround this center, and the Third Aspect was suggested by the narrow outer ring which seems more loosely woven. The whole figure is pervaded by the usual golden light gleaming out between the lines of violet.

The Sevenfold Manifestation.—In all religions there remains some tradition of the great truth that the LOGOS manifests Himself through seven mighty channels, often regarded as minor Logoi or great planetary Spirits. In the Christian scheme they appear as the seven great archangels, sometimes called the seven spirits before the throne of God. The figure numbered 47 shows the result of the effort to meditate upon this method of divine manifestation. We have the golden glow in the center, and also (though with lesser splendor) pervading the form. The line is blue, and it draws a succession of seven graceful and almost featherlike double wings which surround the central glory and are clearly intended as a part of it. As the thought strengthens and expands, these beautiful wings change their color to violet and become like the petals of a flower, and overlap one another in an intricate but exceedingly effective pattern. This gives us a very interesting glimpse into the formation and growth of these shapes in higher matter.

Intellectual Aspiration.—The form depicted in Fig. 43 bears a certain resemblance to that in Fig. 15;

but, beautiful as that was, this is in reality a far higher and grander thought. Here we have a great clear-cut spear or pencil of the pure pale violet which indicates devotion to the highest ideal, and it is outlined and strengthened by an exceedingly fine manifestation of the noblest development of intellect. It will be noted that in both the colors there is a strong admixture of the white light which always indicates unusual spiritual power.

Surely the study of these thought-forms should be a most impressive object-lesson, since from it we may see both what to avoid and what to cultivate, and may learn by degrees to appreciate how tremendous is our responsibility for the exercise of this mighty power. Indeed it is terribly true, as we said in the beginning, that thoughts are things, and puissant things; and it behoves us to remember that every one of us is generating them unceasingly night and day. See how great is the happiness this knowledge brings to us, and how gloriously we can utilize it when we know of some one in sorrow or in suffering. Often circumstances arise which prevent us from giving physical help either by word or deed, however much we may desire to do so; but there is no case in which help by thought may not be given, and no case in which it can fail to produce a definite result. It may often happen that at the moment our friend may be too entirely occupied with his own suffering, or perhaps too much excited, to receive and accept any suggestion from without, but presently a time comes when our thought-form can penetrate and discharge itself, and then assuredly our sympathy will produce its due result. It is indeed true that the responsibility of using such a power is great, yet we should not shrink from our duty on that account. It is sadly true that there are many men who are unconsciously using their thought-power chiefly for evil, yet this only makes it all the more necessary that those of us who are beginning to understand life a little should use it consciously, and use it for good. We have at our command a never-failing criterion; we can never misuse this mighty power of thought if we employ it always in unison with the great divine scheme of evolution, and for the uplifting of our fellow-man.

HELPFUL THOUGHTS

The Figures numbered 48 to 54 were the results of a systematic attempt to send helpful thought by the friend who has furnished us with the sketches. A definite time was given each day at a fixed hour. The forms were in some cases seen by the transmitter, but in all cases were preceived by the recipient, who immediately sent rough sketches of what was seen by the next post to the transmitter, who has kindly supplied the following notes with regard to them:—

" In the colored drawings appended the blue features appear to have represented the more devotional element of the thought. The yellow forms accompanied the endeavor to communicate intellectual fortitude, or mental strength and courage. The rosy pink appeared when the thought was blended with affectionate sympathy. If the sender (A) could formulate his thought deliberately at the appointed time, the receiver (B) would report seeing a large clear form as in Figs. 48, 49, and 54. The latter persisted for some minutes, constantly streaming its luminous yellow ' message ' upon B. If, however, A was of necessity experimenting under difficulty—say walking out of doors—he would occasionally see his ' forms ' broken up into smaller globes, or shapes, such as 50, 51, 52, and B would report their receipt so broken up. In this way many details could be checked and compared as from opposite ends of the line, and the nature of the influence communicated offered another means of verification. Upon one occasion A was disturbed in his endeavor to send a thought of the blue-pink connotation, by a feeling of anxiety that the nature of the pink element should not be misapprehended. The report of B was that a well-defined globe as in Fig. 54 was first seen, but that this suddenly disappeared, being replaced by a moving procession of little light-green triangles, as in Fig. 53. These few drawings give but a slight idea of the varied flower-like and geometric forms seen, while neither paint nor crayon-work seems capable of representing the glowing beauty of their living colors."

Forms Built by Music

Before closing this little treatise it will perhaps be of interest to our readers to give a few examples of another type of forms. Many people are aware that sound is always associated with color—that when, for example, a musical note is sounded, a flash of color corresponding to it may be seen by those whose finer senses are already to some extent developed. It seems not to be so generally known that sound produces form as well as color, and that every piece of music leaves behind it an impression of this nature, which persists for some considerable time, and is clearly visible and intelligible to those who have eyes to see. Such a shape is perhaps not technically a thought-form—unless indeed we take it, as we well may, as the result of the thought of the composer expressed by means of the skill of the musician through his instrument.

Some such forms are very striking and impressive, and naturally their variety is infinite. Each class of music has its own type of form, and the style of the composer shows as clearly in the form which his music builds as a man's character shows in his handwriting. Other possibilities of variation are introduced by the kind of instrument upon which the music is performed, and also by the merits of the player. The same piece of music if accurately played will always build the same form, but that form will be enormously larger when it is played upon a church organ or by a military band than when it is performed upon a piano, and not only the size but also the texture of the resultant form will be very different. There will also be a similar difference in texture between the result of a piece of music played upon a violin and the same piece executed upon the flute. Again, the excellence of the performance has its effect, and there is a wonderful difference between the radiant beauty of the form produced by the work of a true artist, perfect alike in expression and execution and the comparatively dull and undistinguished-looking one which represents the effort of the wooden and mechanical player. Anything like inaccuracy in rendering naturally leaves a corresponding defect in form, so that the exact character of the performance shows itself just as clearly to the clairvoyant spectator as it does to the auditor.

It is obvious that, if time and capacity permitted, hundreds of volumes might be filled with drawings of the forms built by different pieces of music under different conditions, so that the most that can be done within any reasonable compass is to give a few examples of the leading types. It has been decided for the purposes of this book to limit these to three, to take types of music presenting readily recognizable contrasts, and for the sake of simplicity in comparison to present them all as they appeared when played upon the same instrument—a very fine church organ. In each of our Plates the church shows as well as the thought-form which towers far into the air above it; and it should be remembered that though the drawings are on very different scales the church is the same in all three cases, and consequently the relative size of the sound-form can easily be calculated. The actual height of the tower of the church is just under a hundred feet, so it will be seen that the sound-form produced by a powerful organ is enormous in size.

Such forms remain as coherent erections for some considerable time—an hour or two at least; and during all that time they are radiating forth their characteristic vibrations in every direction, just as our thought-forms do; and if the music be good, the effect of those vibrations cannot but be uplifting to every man upon whose vehicles they play. Thus the community owes a very real debt of gratitude to the musician who pours forth such helpful influences, for he may affect for good hundreds whom he never saw and will never know upon the physical plane.

Mendelssohn.—The first of such forms, a comparatively small and simple one, is drawn for us in Plate M. It will be seen that we have here a shape roughly representing that of a balloon, having a scalloped outline consisting of a double violet line. Within that there is an arrangement of variously-colored lines moving almost parallel with this outline; and then another somewhat similar arrangement which seems to cross and interpenetrate the first. Both of these sets of lines evidently start from the organ within the church, and consequently pass upward through its roof in their course, physical matter being clearly no obstacle to their formation. In the hollow center of the form float a number of small crescents arranged apparently in four vertical lines.

Let us endeavor now to give some clue to the meaning of all this, and to explain in some measure how it comes into existence. It must be recollected that this is a melody of simple character played once thıough, and that consequently we can analyse the form in a way that would be quite impossible with a larger and more complicated specimen. Yet even in this case we cannot give all the details, as will presently be seen. Disregarding for the moment the scalloped border, we have next within it an arrangement of four lines of different colors running in the same direction, the outermost being blue and the others crimson, yellow and green respectively. These lines are exceedingly irregular and crooked; in fact, they each consist of a number of short lines at various levels joined together perpendicularly. It seems that each of these short lines represents a note of music, and that the irregularity of their arrangement indicates the succession of these notes; so that each of these crooked lines signifies the movement of one of the parts of the melody, the four moving approximately together denoting the treble, alto, tenor and bass respectively, though they do not necessarily appear in that order in this astral form. Here it is necessary to interpolate a still further explanation. Even with a melody so comparatively simple as this there are tints and shades far too finely modulated to be reproduced on any scale at all within our reach; therefore it must be said that each of the short lines expressing a note has a color of its own, so that although as a whole that outer line gives an impression of blueness, and the one next within it of carmine,

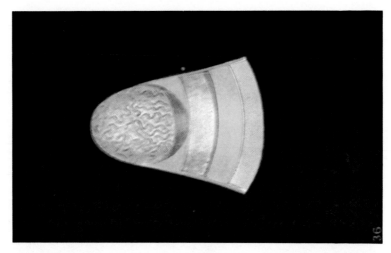

36

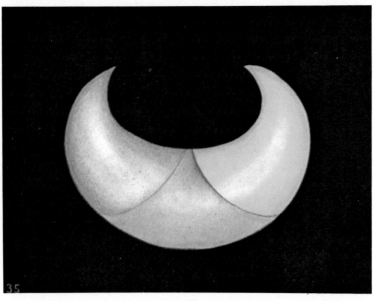

35

37

39

40

41

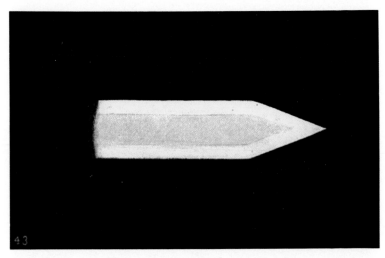

43

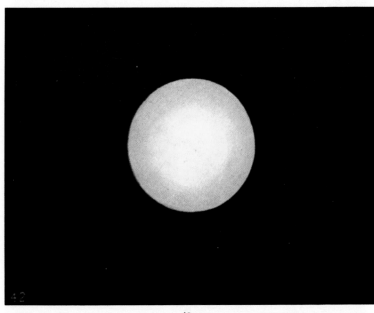

42

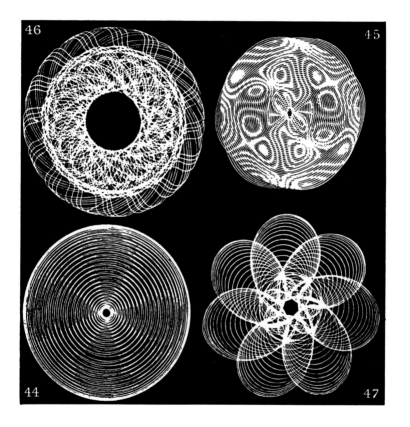

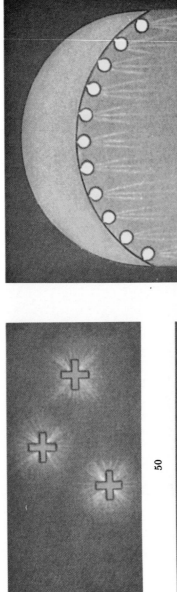

50

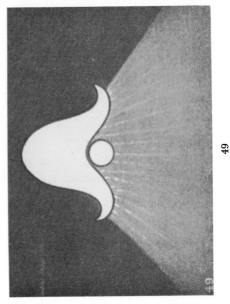

49

48

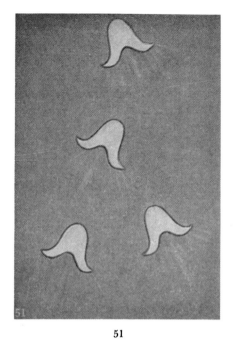

51

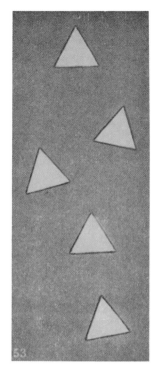

53

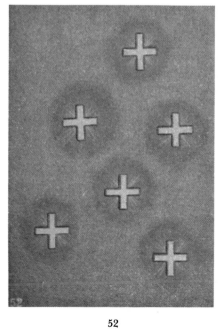

52

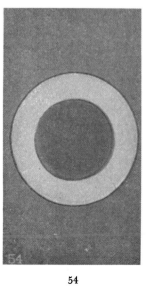

54

M

G

W

each yet varies in every inch of its length; so that what is shown is not a correct reproduction of every tint, but only the general impression.

The two sets of four lines which seem to cross one another are caused by two sections of the melody; the scalloped edging surrounding the whole is the result of various flourishes and arpeggios, and the floating crescents in the centre represent isolated or staccato chords. Naturally the arpeggios are not wholly violet for each loop has a different hue, but on the whole they approach more nearly to that color than to any other. The height of this form above the tower of the church is probably a little over a hundred feet; but since it also extends downward through the roof of the church its total perpendicular diameter may well be about a hundred and fifty feet. It is produced by one of Mendelssohn's " Lieder ohne Wörte ", and is characteristic of the delicate filigree-work which so often appears as the result of his compositions.

The whole form is seen projected against a coruscating background of many colors, which is in reality a cloud surrounding it upon every side, caused by the vibrations which are pouring out from it in all directions.

◀━━━━━━━━━━━━━━━━━━

MUSICAL THOUGHT-FORMS

The music played on the organ was:

(Plate "M") *Mendelssohn*: No. 9 of his "Songs without words".
(Plate "G") *Gounod*: Soldiers Chorus from "Faust".
(Plate "W") *Wagner*: Overture to "The Meistersingers".

Gounod.—In Plate G we have an entirely different piece—a ringing chorus by Gounod. Since the church in the illustration is the same, it is easy to calculate that in this case the highest point of the form must rise fully six hundred feet above the tower, though the perpendicular diameter of the form is somewhat less than that, for the organist has evidently finished some minutes ago, and the perfected shape floats high in the air, clearly defined and roughly spherical, though rather an oblate spheroid. This spheroid is hollow, as are all such forms, for it is slowly increasing in size—gradually radiating outward from its center, but growing proportionately less vivid and more ethereal in appearance as it does so, until at last it loses coherence and fades away much as a wreath of smoke might do. The golden glory surrounding and interpenetrating it indicates as before the radiation of its vibrations, which in this case show the dominant yellow in much greater proportion than did Mendelssohn's gentler music.

The coloring here is far more brilliant and massive than in Plate M, for this music is not so much a thread of murmurous melody as a splendid succession of crashing chords. The artist has sought to give the effect of the chords rather than that of the separate notes, the latter being scarcely possible on a scale so small as this. It is therefore more difficult here to follow the development of the form, for in this much longer piece the lines have crossed and intermingled, until we have little but the gorgeous general effect

which the composer must have intended us to feel
—and to see, if we were able to see. Nevertheless
it is possible to discern something of the process
which builds the form, and the easiest point at which
to commence is the lowest on the left hand as one
examines the Plate. The large violet protrusion there
is evidently the opening chord of a phrase, and if
we follow the outer line of the form upward and
round the circumference we may obtain some idea
of the character of that phrase. A close inspection
will reveal two other lines further in which run roughly
parallel to this outer one, and show similar succession
of color on a smaller scale, and these may well
indicate a softer repetition of the same phrase.

Careful analysis of this nature will soon convince
us that there is a very real order in this seeming chaos,
and we shall come to see that if it were possible to
make a reproduction of this glowing glory that should
be accurate down to the smallest detail, it would also
be possible patiently to disentangle it to the utter-
most, and to assign every lovely touch of coruscating color to the very note that called it into existence.
It must not be forgotten that very far less detail is
given in this illustration than in Plate M; for example,
each of these points or projections has within it as
integral parts, at least the four lines or bands of varying color which were shown as separate in Plate M,
but here they are blended into one shade, and only
the general effect of the chord is given. In M we
combined horizontally, and tried to show the charac-

teristics of a number of succession notes blended into one, but to keep distinct the effect of the four simultaneous parts by using a differently-colored line for each. In G we attempt exactly the reverse, for we combine vertically, and blend, not the successive notes of one part, but the chords, each probably containing six or eight notes. The true appearance combines these two effects with an inexpressible wealth of detail.

Wagner.—No one who has devoted any study to these musical forms would hesitate in ascribing the marvellous mountain-range depicted in Plate W to the genius of Richard Wagner, for no other composer has yet built sound edifices with such power and decision. In this case we have a vast bell-shaped erection, fully nine hundred feet in height, and but little less in diameter at the bottom, floating in the air above the church out of which it has arisen. It is hollow, like Gounod's form, but, unlike that, it is open at the bottom. The resemblance to the successively retreating ramparts of a mountain is almost perfect, and it is heightened by the billowy masses of cloud which roll between the crags and give the effect of perspective. No attempt has been made in this drawing to show the effect of single notes or single chords; each range of mimic rocks represents in size, shape and color only the general effect of one of the sections of the piece of music as seen from a distance. But it must be understood that in reality both this and the form given in Plate G are as full of minute details as that depicted in Plate M, and that all these magnificent masses of color are built up of many comparatively small bands which would not be separately visible upon the scale on which this is drawn. The broad result is that each mountain-peak has its own brilliant hue, just as it is seen in the illustration— a splendid splash of vivid color, glowing with the glory of its own living light, spreading its resplendent radiance over all the country round. Yet in each of these masses of color other colors are constantly flickering, as they do over the surface of molten metal, so that the coruscations and scintillations of these wondrous astral edifices are far beyond the power of any physical words to describe.

A striking feature in this form is the radical difference between the two types of music which occur in it, one producing the angular rocky masses, and the other the rounded billowy clouds which lie between them. Other *motifs* are shown by the broad bands of blue and rose and green which appear at the base of the bell, and the meandering lines of white and yellow which quiver across them are probably produced by a rippling arpeggio accompaniment.

In these three Plates only the form created directly by the sound-vibrations has been drawn, though as seen by the clairvoyant it is usually surrounded by many other minor forms, the result of the personal feelings of the performer or of the emotions aroused among the audience by the music. To recapitulate briefly: in Plate M we have a small and comparatively simple form portrayed in considerable detail, something of the effect of each note being given; in Plate G we have a more elaborate form of very different character delineated with less detail, since no attempt is made to render the separate notes, but only to show how each chord expresses itself in form and color; in Plate W we have a still greater and richer form, in the depiction of which all detail is avoided, in order that the full effect of the piece as a whole may be approximately given.

Naturally every sound makes its impression upon astral and mental matter—not only those ordered successions of sounds which we call music. Some day, perhaps, the forms built by those other less euphonious sounds may be pictured for us, though they are beyond the scope of this treatise; meantime, those who feel an interest in them may read an account of them in the book on *The Hidden Side of Things*.[1]

It is well for us ever to bear in mind that there is a hidden side to life—that each act and word and thought has its consequence in the unseen world which is always so near to us, and that usually these unseen results are of infinitely greater importance than those which are visible to all upon the physical plane. The wise man, knowing this, orders his life accordingly, and takes account of the whole of the world in which he lives, and not of the outer husk of it only. Thus he saves himself an infinity of trouble, and makes his

[1] By C. W. Leadbeater.

life not only happier but far more useful to his fellow-men. But to do this implies knowledge—that knowledge which is power.

To exist is not enough; we desire to live intelligently. But to live we must know, and to know we must study; and here is a vast field open before us, if we will only enter upon it and gather the fruits of that Divine Wisdom which in these modern days men call Theosophy.